Copyright © 1985 Concordia Publishing House
3558 S. Jefferson Avenue, St. Louis, MO 63118-3968
Manufactured in the United States of America

Library of Congress Cataloging in Publication Data

Schilder, Joyce, 1952-
  Abram talked with God.

  (God's little learner series)
  Summary: Retells the Old Testament story of Abraham and how he came to talk with God.
  1. Abraham (Biblical patriarch)—Juvenile literature. 2. God—Juvenile literature. |1. Abraham (Biblical patriarch) 2. Bible stories—O.T.| I. Title. II. Series.
BS580.A3S36   1985   222'.110924   85-7763
ISBN 0-570-08950-6

1 2 3 4 5 6 7 8 9 10   DP   94 93 92 91 90 89 88 87 86 85

There was once a man named Abram.
He lived with his wife, Sarai, in a
land called Haran.

Abram was a farmer. He took care
of dogs and goats and sheep
and cattle.
He was a good farmer.

And Abram did one other thing
very, very well.

He listened.

He listened to the birds sing,
and he listened to the water ripple.

He listened to the bees buzz,
and he listened to the fire crackle.

And . . .

he listened to the quiet.

Shh-h-h-h.

One day Abram was sitting alone
under an old, old tree
when he heard a voice.
"Abram," said the voice.

"Who's there?" he asked
as he jumped to his feet.
He looked all around.
"Where are You?" Abram asked.

"I am here," said the voice,
"but you can't see Me.
You must sit very still and listen.
Please, don't be afraid."

Abram was afraid,
but he sat down and listened very hard.

"I am the Lord, your God," said the voice.
"I have come to make a promise to you.
I will give you many children and grandchildren.
I will make your name great.
I will bless you.
And I will bless other people through you.
But . . .

"First you must move your family to a place
that I will show you.
You must do as I say."

Abram was still a little scared.
He looked around with wonder and amazement.
Abram cleared his throat
and said in a great big voice,

"Yes, Lord."

And from that day on,
Abram talked with God.

THE END

Dorothy Van Woerkom helps children personally relate to the true meaning of Christmas and Christianity with her writing. Her previously published children's books include *Stepka*, *The Dove and the Messiah*, and *Journeys to Bethlehem*. Ms. Van Woerkom is also the series editor for *I Can Read a Bible Story*.

Art Kirchhoff is a staff artist for Concordia Publishing House and a graduate of Washington Universtity, School of Fine Arts. He and his wife, Ruth, and their three daughters reside in St. Louis, Mo.